GARY BANKS AND EDDIE KINLEY, JR.

SHARING CHRIST with BLACK MUSLIMS

An Introducti
the Orien

Black Muslims

Published by **BKin Light Ministries**

Published by
BKin Light Ministries
6 Woodland Drive
Bridgeton, NJ 08302
(609) 451-3226

Edited by Terry V. Thomas
Designed by SQUARE 1 STUDIO
Type set: 12/16 Journal Text
All Bible texts are taken from the KJV. Copyright.

Certificate of Registration TXu639-347

PRINTED IN CANADA

ACKNOWLEDGEMENTS

The Bible is clear. Jesus said in John 12:32, "If I be lifted up I will draw all men unto me." That text became more clear to me when I met four men searching for the truth. They were studying independently, looking for a way out of all the religious confusion. I want to take the time to thank them for their diligent search and study for the truth. Rick, Greg, Ric-Ric, and Richard. They thought they found everything they need in Islam, but the Holy Spirit led them to the church I was pastoring. I'm so glad that the Lord saw fit to allow me to be the one to baptize them into Christianity. Black Muslims can be reached, but only if Jesus is lifted up in His True Light. Not the light of anyone else.

Thanks also to Bruce Bauer at the SDA Theological Seminary who got excited about our independent study and encouraged us to continue our research after graduation.

During the 1930's, Elijah Muhammad found-
ed a Black religious movement in Detroit,
Michigan. Known as the Nation of Islam or Black
Muslims, this small band of believers took their
theology from a combination of traditional Islam,
Black nationalist perspectives on history, and the
unique teachings of Mr. Muhammad. While large
Black Christian congregations of the northeastern
United States took little notice, the Nation of Islam
delivered a blistering critique of Christians and
Christian churches that tolerated racism and
upheld the oppressors of Black people. Years later,
even as Martin Luther King Jr. and scores of
Christian clergymen mounted a frontal attack on
racism, the Nation of Islam amassed a membership
in the tens of thousands, and its the dynamic
spokesman, Malcolm X, continued the critique of
traditional Christian churches before a national
audience.

Confronted by a direct challenge to their
mission, Christians in Black communities around
the nation reassessed their witness to their communities. Had they been attentive to the physical
needs of their neighbors? Had they addressed the
issues of racism, discrimination, blight, poverty,
broken homes and violence? Had they really been
a "light" in their communities, or had they simply

opened their doors for a once-a-week fellowship with their own circle of believers.

I see SHARING CHRIST WITH BLACK MUSLIMS as an outcome of that reassessment. It is the first to help Christians who seek to understand the attraction of the Black Muslims to the Black masses, and to offer concrete ways for Christians to develop an effective witness to Black Muslims.

We live in a world where many ideas compete. True believers in the teaching of Jesus will welcome an opportunity to witness to their neighbors of all faiths, not in a spirit of competition, but because the joy that Jesus brings must be expressed in witnessing.

Emory J. Tolbert
Chairman
Department of History
Howard University

CONTENTS

introduction

The Challenge of Spreading the Gospel

There is a great commission given by Jesus to his disciples. He told them, "Go ye into all the world, and preach the gospel to every creature" (Mark 16:15). This commission became the model for Christians to establish a system for outreach to every part of the world attempting to reach every culture, and every people group in the world.

For the first disciples the task may have seemed insurmountable. A small band of men and women determined to spread the news of Jesus Christ to the then known world. The only vehicles to spread such a message were the written word and word of mouth. Even with these two limited resources the news spread quickly.

Today across the globe there exist approximately 15,000 languages with over 30,000 dialects.

The task is as great now as it was then. But with advances in communication and transportation the word can spread more quickly.

Radio waves can be picked up thousands of miles away; church missionary projects are getting pass language barriers by the gifts of interpretation. There are no limits to our mission outreach. The Church is preaching the gospel message in thousands of languages and dialects. Even what used to be the Soviet Union is now open to Christianity.

Despite the great strides in the world, there is one people group we have failed to reach in our own backyard. We cannot afford to overlook any people group. We must find a remedy for this problem if we are to complete the mission.

Our lack of success in reaching this people group is mainly because no organized outreach has been provided to them. Why have we been unable to reach them? Is it because we cannot find them? No! We can't claim inaccessibility as the problem because they are standing on many street corners in the inner-cities. Is the problem a language barrier? No! We can't claim language barriers because their tongue is our tongue. We can't claim that we don't have anything to share because Christ is the greatest truth of all.

Christians have penetrated every continent in the world. Our missionaries have reached many people groups across the globe in several languages.[1] Even with the wide range of languages, ninety-two per cent of the world has access to some portion of the scriptures in their mother tongue. Ninety per cent of the world has access to the Bible in some understood language. Eighty-five per cent of the world has access to the whole Bible in their mother tongue. There are 550 new translations for languages that have not been available in the past decade.[2]

Christians have improved their outreach efforts because of technological advances, the use of media, and the translation of foreign languages and dialects. In spite of these improvements, Christians have overlooked an outreach to Black Muslims. One could argue that the problem is fear of the unknown. Too few Christians in America know anything about Black Muslims. This is the motivation behind **Sharing Christ with Black Muslims**. With this information, we must get busy before it is too late.

chapter 1

The Black Muslim Movement

Black Muslims practice a religion known as Islam. The most visible sect of Black Muslims is the Nation of Islam. The Nation of Islam, or otherwise referred to as the Nation, is one of many sects of Black Muslims. It is the sect that is most nationalistic in nature. It should be noted here that there are other Muslims who are Black, but dissociate themselves from the Nation. Furthermore, all Black Muslim groups find their origin in the Nation of Islam.

Exactly when the Movement began remains a mystery. Founded by the Prophet W. D. Fard, he led the Nation in the early nineteen-thirties. According to legend, Fard came from Arabia and was Allah incarnate.

His organization first concentrated on

Detroit Negroes and gained an estimated membership of perhaps 8,000 during the critical years of the Great Depression. Late in 1933, Fard mysteriously disappeared and Elijah Muhammad became the leader of the Movement as instructed by Fard. Fard apparently observed that Elijah Muhammad possessed all the qualities of a great leader.

Elijah Muhammad began working with zeal, leading men and women to Islam. He taught and instructed them that they were the original, superior race created by Allah. Elijah Muhammad informed his followers that they must take back their rightful place as princes and kings of the earth. The Nation appealed to many Negroes. Within time, their success and popularity began to turn heads all across America. Today they continue to grow at an alarming rate under the leadership of Minister Louis Farakahn.

During the Civil Rights Movement the Black Muslims found little support. Much of Black America distanced themselves from what was to them a doctrine of hate. The cry was reverse discrimination, but this was hardly an accurate description of the teachings of the Nation. It had been too long before the members of the Black Community began to vent their frustrations, and the Nation caused this ideology.

"The Nation of Islam is important not because it tells whites how bitterly Negroes feel about their present conditions, but for showing the Negro masses 'why' they feel the way they do, 'how' they may get out of their degradation, and 'how' they may become self-respecting citizens."[3]

The Nation..."was undeniably a mass movement. They are reaching for the support of the entire Black lower-class and, ultimately, of all Black Americans."[4] The movement exploded because of the disparity in equality for the Black Man.

Many Movements in America raised the awareness of Blacks. No other Movement opened the eyes of the Black Community as did the Nation. There has always been a dichotomy in the Black Community about equality. Some Blacks always have and always will believe that they are treated well. Others believe that they have been oppressed. The Black Muslims have attempted to show the Black Community that Black people don't deserve to be treated unfairly. They have preached equality and they have attacked oppression. Despite their attempts, the dichotomy remains with the Black Community.

To demonstrate this dichotomy let us look at the differences between the house Negro and the field Negro. The field Negroes saw the master for what he was. He was made to work under extreme adverse conditions. The house Negro, on the other hand, had it easy. They served the master in the house and got the best scraps from dinner.

There have always been a limited number of house Negroes and an abundance of field Negroes. House Negroes have forgotten about the field Negroes. House Negroes believed that freedom was unreasonable, they thought they had it all. They worked in the master's house, served the master's food, raised the master's children, and shined the master's shoes. They believed this was the "good life", and they equated this "good life" with freedom.

The house Negroes were selected because they were loyal to the master. The master never had to worry about a rebellion from the house Negro. In fact being selected as a house Negro was a reward. When the master was convinced that this slave would not embarrass him or would act like a "good nigger" they could be a house Negro.

Some things haven't changed much. Today, the field Negroes are trying to tell the house Negroes that just because you have the same education as the master, work the same place as the master, live on the same side of the railroad tracks

as the master, have the same kind of car as the
master, and your children go to the same school as
the master's—doesn't mean that you have the same
privileges as the master. The field Negroes have
been trying to convince the house Negroes that
freedom is better than slavery regardless of the
century.

Black Muslims would consider themselves as
modern day field Negroes. These modern day field
Negroes have been trying to tell the modern day
house Negroes that there are better opportunities
for the Black Man.

Black Muslims are not, however, the first
group of field Negroes to raise the consciousness of
the modern day house Negroes. Many Black leaders wielded the sword of Black consciousness during slavery and in the days following the
Emancipation Proclamation. "One century after the
Emancipation Proclamation we are still trying to
repair the moral ravages of slavery. Our progress
is slow and sluggish. It is this sluggishness that
has given rise to the melodramatic Black Muslim
Movement."[5]

Some nationalist would argue that one of
the major reasons for this sluggishness may be
attributed to the short-sightedness of the Black
Church in America. We will deal with this in

more detail in chapter two.

The membership of the Nation is made up of mostly Black Men. Muslims have displayed an uncanny ability to reach Black Men when they are at their lowest point in life. They have reformed the criminal, educated the unlearned, liberated the illiterate, and changed the thinking of Black Men. Black Men who become Muslims think more positively than they did before becoming Muslim.

Before joining the Nation many of these men were drug addicts and drunks making little or no contribution to society. Their lifestyle marred their identity. That's when the Nation is at its best. They invade the slums and penetrate the crack houses with a message of hope. The result, reformed men leading productive lives and their hope is no longer on holiday. Many Muslims experience such situations.

When one reaches the fruition of his religious beliefs, a metamorphosis has been completed. He is quite impressive with his knowledge of scripture, the Koran, and pertinent social and religious issues. At this stage of his experience there is very little one can do to challenge his theology.

These are some of the issues that the Black Muslims deal with.

chapter 2

The Church, The Community, The Nation

Christians have not been successful in reaching the members of the Nation. There is a certain amount of mystery surrounding it. Black Christian Churches in the inner-city have only recently begun paying attention to the activity of the Black Muslims. Black Muslims are moving in on ministries that the Black Church used to provide. The Black Church used to represent the masses. Now it appears that the Black Church has created its own status quo. Unless the church does something about something about it, the Nation will soon replace the Black Church as the official representative for the Black Community.

An increased awareness of the conditions of the Black Community has raised the interest of many Black clergy, including the authors, in the Black Muslim movement. The Black Community has fallen victim to various social ills and conditions that the Christian Church, with few exceptions, has failed to address effectively. Both local and the national government have developed entitlement programs to curtail some of these issues. The question that has been posed is, have these programs hurt or helped our community?

Who controls the destiny of the Black Man and his community? The Nation believes that the destiny of the Black Man is in his own hands. That's why Minister Louis Farakahn organized the Million Man March on Washington, on October 16, 1995. This march demonstrated unity among Black Men. Several Black leaders had a problem with the march because it was organized by Farakahn. There was some suspicion about whether or not Farakahn was trying to promote himself or the Nation. The march proved otherwise. There were, however, many national leaders from the Black Community that participated in this march. The Muslims showed that they were more interested in motivating Black Men to action.

There is no other group that could have

drawn over a million Black Men for a march on Washington. The Muslims are very influential in the Black Community. The Christian church used to have the strongest influence in the Community. At the present rate the Nation will soon have that responsibility. They have gained influence on the grass roots level more than any other group.

The Church and the NAACP cannot compete with the Nation. Part of the reason that the Black Church is losing its influence in the community is the unfortunate perception of the Black Clergy.

The general perception of the Black Clergy, as vividly portrayed in the Off Broadway Musical, "The Preacher and the Rapper", is that instead of giving to the community the clergy is taking from the community. Black Clergy should not have to take all of the blame because the mission of the Church has changed. Parishioners have "arrived" at success and forgotten from whence they came. It has taken some time for this to become evident, but now it is clear.

The Black Church used to be a catalyst for change. Through the leadership of the pastor they stood against the terrible ills that surrounded the people of the inner-cities. The Church was a place of refuge and asylum. This is no longer the rule, rather it is now the exception.

Let us remind the reader what Jesus said to the disciples in Matthew 26:11, "For ye have the poor always with you." We celebrate improvement on the quality of life. We must, however, never forget that there will always be poor Black People. The Church must learn to continue its ministry to them although they have gone on to greener pastures.

These are just some reasons that have made many people in the Black Community call the Church a "joke". The Church is challenging fewer social issues. The voice of the Church concerning inequality and racism is just a whisper and as a result we forget the needy. Some of those who have left the Christian Church in search of fulfillment are finding their way to the Black Muslim Movement.

chapter 3

Christianity and Racism

When a Black Man leaves Christianity and goes to Islam it is very difficult to win him back. It is most difficult when the man is searching for liberation. Because the Black Church doesn't emphasize liberation it is difficult for any Christian group to penetrate the Nation. Without an emphasis on liberation, Christianity is viewed as the religion of and for the white man. It is seen as another way for white America to control and limit the social and economic progress of the Black people in America.

On the other hand Muslim theology is a liberation theology and it will not allow its people to accept any form of oppression as the norm. Notice this quote from a term paper that a young Muslim presented for a religion class at Clark University for Professor C. Eric Lincoln:

The Christian religion is incompatible with

the Negro's aspirations for dignity and equality in America. It has hindered where it might have helped; it has been evasive when it was morally bound to be forthright; it has separated believers on the basis of color although it has declared its mission to be a universal brotherhood under Jesus Christ. Christian love is the white man's love for himself and for his race. For the man who is not white, Islam is the hope for justice and equality in the world we must build tomorrow. (Lincoln, C. Eric. *The Black Muslims in America.* Westport, Connecticut: Green Wood Press, 1973.)

This statement holds within it the basic premise that Black Muslims espouse against Christianity. We have found some truth in their teachings against racism; but what is the real issue? Is it Christianity or racism that disgusts Black Muslims? Have the brothers and sisters of Islam confused the two? Perhaps what we are really looking at is the behavior of people who claim Christianity. Black Muslims have developed such an apathy toward Christianity because of what they consider being its racist history.

There is no denying that people who claim Christianity have fallen short of the righteousness of God. People will always come up short; what we want Black Muslims to realize is that you cannot judge Christ by Christians. Christ is the only standard by which Christianity may be measured; all else is incomplete.

We are living in a day when it is socially acceptable to be a Christian. So many have taken on the name of Christian, but fail to meet the standards of Christianity. Black Muslims have seen the actions of the members of the Church and the history of the Church and rejected Christ. They see Christianity as oppressive for in the Dark Ages men and women were denied equality because of their belief system. They see Christianity as oppressive because countless massacres were done in the name of the Church. The Church allowed these atrocities in order to meet the selfish ends of man.

Anyone who sees Christianity as oppressive is wrong, to the contrary, Christianity is liberating. It was Jesus who spoke these liberating words, "The Spirit of the Lord is upon me, because he hath anointed me to preach the gospel to the poor; he hath sent me to heal the brokenhearted, to preach deliverance to the captives and recovering of sight to the blind, to set at liberty them that are bruised" (Luke 4:18). Christ teaches liberation. Christians

have failed but Christ never fails. Don't judge
Christ by Christians.

Many things that Muslims teach about
Christianity are ridiculous. You should, however,
be prepared for the degree of accuracy you will
discover as you read. If you think that Western
Christianity is pure and flawless you might not be
ready to read the allegations the Muslims make
against it.

Seeing some of the ills that have become
commonplace in western society would help us to
identify with the morality issue that Black Muslims
hold against Christianity. If we believe that all
things are fair and just, we are living a fairy tale
existence and will make a poor candidate to reach
Black Muslims.

If you have ever talked with a Black Muslim
you will discover that they know the scriptures as
well as, if not better than, most Christians. Black
Muslims are very studious with the Bible and the
Koran. This is why it is so difficult to witness to
them. They are generally very patient when they
speak to you about Christianity, but they do not
trust the white man who claims Christianity.
That's why Christians must emphasize Christ and
not Christianity.

Distrust has been for so long ingrained in

the mind of the Black Muslim that it is difficult to have an open-minded discussion with them. Black Muslims give few opportunities for open discussion especially with men that they perceive to have little knowledge of the social environment. The task of convincing a Black Muslim to convert to Christianity is exceptionally difficult. There is an element that as Christians we have in our favor, and that is the wooing work of the Holy Spirit.

A witness loses ground when he proves himself oblivious to the inequities perpetuated upon the masses in America and throughout the world. The reason for this is that Black Muslims have an outreach program that presupposes Islam as the only religion for the Black Man. Islam sees every Black Man as..."the mighty, the wise, the best but do not know it. Being without the knowledge we disgrace ourselves...[Islam calls for Black Men]...to give up the white race's name and religion in order to gain success."[6]

chapter 4

The Profile and the Stages

There are stages to the Muslim lifestyle that can be paralleled to any other religious experience. Each stage becomes increasingly difficult for the Christian to reach Black Muslims. We are trying to discover at what stage we can effectively help the Black Muslim make the transfer from Islam to Christianity. Our goal is to provide a positive way of life that can be fulfilling to them with their present view of society, while giving them a new view of Christianity.

Before introducing the stages, we want to give a profile of the young Black Man headed for the Nation. This will help you understand their view of society and Christianity. This is an example of what kinds of experiences men go through and how one might develop such a mentality that would make Islam appeal to them.

Many Black Men who become Muslims initially find Islam in the prison system. When a man accepts Islam while in prison he is usually doing so to be part of a support group. Most Black Men in prison find support in the Muslim religion. Most of these men are in it because they find protection, fellowship and a sense of belonging, something they have not seen in Christianity.

Observe this scenario found in many homes where we find a juvenile delinquent. Here we see a young man in his teens living in the meager shelter provided by his parents. The two bedroom apartment located on the fifth floor project building makes him sick. This young man finds himself bombarded with questions concerning equality and self-respect.

School has become a drag. Evidently most of his white teachers care little or nothing about his intellectual progress nor his social and emotional development. Affirmation comes not from within the classroom but on the streets. If he is lucky he may graduate, but with a poor grade point average. His self-esteem and pride have been robbed, then he turns to his only source of strength, his "boys".

Before long he is on the corner selling drugs

or carjacking. With a pocket full of money he stalks the neighborhood as if he is king of the jungle. He swears to his mother that he will retire when he has enough money to move them out of the ragged community.

His mother, a devout Christian, has never received any help from the church with the raising of her son. Church members will ridicule her if she is not part of their inner circle. So she keeps her mouth shut and continually makes excuses to the pastor for her son's absence. With no help at home and no help from the Church she turns to her only friend, Jesus. Her knees are worn out and her pillow soaked with tears as she confesses her negligence. "Oh Lord, where did I go wrong with my boy?" He arrives home late some nights as his mother prays to an unseen God. He mocks the God he thinks has been so hard on the Black Man and so easy on his white counterpart.

This example greatly affects the psyche of the young man. When he finally gets caught by the police, he blames his mother's God for not protecting him. He resolves in his mind that he will not be a Christian. Why should he? In his mind God doesn't hear his mother's prayers.

The next step for this young man is to go through the justice system. He is arrested and probably beaten by police who are white, he is given a white court appointed attorney who has very little interest in his destiny. He appeals to a white judge who places a heavier sentence on him because he is Black. He sees the white criminals who have committed worse crimes get less time. The jury who convicts him is mostly, if not all, white. He finds himself in prison in which mostly Black Men reside and are guarded by white men with shot guns."[7]

At this point in his life he has built a negative image of the white man. Then it happens, members of the Nation approach him and instruct him about his oppression. Other Muslims instruct him concerning the will of Allah, and within months he has become indoctrinated.

These are the elements of society that make the message of Islam so appealing to a man plagued by negative societal issues all of his life. This makes it simple to be won to Islam. An anti-establishment religion appeals to an incarcerated man. An anti-Christian religion appeals to a man who sees Christianity as a defective religion. An anti-white religion appeals to a man who has witnessed the oppression of his people left to struggle in a white man's world. They tell him the white man is the devil and he accepts it. This is the **EMBITTERED STAGE.**

In the embittered stage a young man in not very receptive to religion. He doesn't see the reality of Christianity in his life now. He cannot be told that Jesus is going to make it all better. He has gone through a traumatic experience. Jesus had his chance and he blew it. He sees Jesus in everything that is against him. The teachings of Islam support this.

At this stage the young man is filled with animosity. His emotions get the best of him. He fails to think rationally. He hates white people and any representation of white people, namely Christianity. The embittered stage is followed by the **INTRODUCTORY STAGE**.

One of the Muslims brothers will try to reason with him. At first he doesn't want to hear it. As they talk, racism is explained to him. He sees that there is a group of people who are trying to combat the racism in America. His interest is slowly kindled and he accepts the teachings. He realized that what they were teaching was true. He wants to learn more and takes a natural progression to the **PUPIL STAGE**.

In the pupil stage he becomes a student and the teachings of Islam help him to cope with the reality of the world around him. The teachings of Islam show the young Black Man why he is where he is, without condemning him. Christians often find themselves condemning young Black Men. While the Nation does not condemn him, it does, however, take advantage of the vulnerability of young men who fit the profile. At first Islam is more of a social movement than a religious one.

Eventually things change, the pupil changes. The teachings of Islam induce a transformation process that reveals to its pupils the evil practices of the white man throughout history.

Suddenly the pupil awakens and becomes conscious for the first time. It all makes sense, slavery, the Civil Rights Movement, the philosophies of the Black Panthers and other Black Power Movements. He becomes aware of the presence and tactics of his enemies and soon his hatred will be channeled in a more disciplined and productive avenue.

The new Muslim will remain in the pupil stage until he comes up for parole. He is equipped with the knowledge gained in prison to combat the evils of society. However, a difficult choice stands in his way. He must find a local mosque and join or abandon his new found faith. Some will not continue in the Muslim tradition when they come out of prison. He may feel that religion has served his needs while he was in prison. Sadly enough, if this is his decision he is likely to return to a life of crime. The committed Muslim, on the other hand, will stay with the Movement and goes on to the **FREEDOM STAGE**.

The freedom stage is relatively short. The decision he makes when he leaves prison determines his success in this stage. They are out on their own, they can no longer hide behind the group. It is in this stage that is the best time to win a Muslim. He is given a new start and the lessons taught on the inside have not been proven on the outside.

Attempts to win a Muslim in this stage would involve the prison chaplain. The authors also maintain that the chaplain should be Black and was capable to relate to him on a level he is familiar with. Black Muslims will not deal with Black Men who are perceived to have assimilated into white culture and forgotten his people.

When these men leave prison the chaplain must be there to help him because if he is not there, the Muslims will be. If he gets in with the Muslims when he gets out he enters the **SERVICE STAGE**.

Those who leave prison and continue in the religion, serve Allah. They learn in the Muslim school systems; they work with Muslims; they live

SHARING CHRIST WITH BLACK MUSLIMS

with Muslims; they begin to have very little contact with the society as we know it. Muslims become self-sufficient and self-contained.

In the service stage he finds that the things that he does for the organization matter. He discovers his contribution counts. This leads him to study on how to be a good Muslim. You have seen young men standing on the street corners selling the Muslim newspaper and bean pies. They are fulfilling a vow of service.

The service stage takes on a natural progression into the **FRUITION STAGE**. It should be emphasized that the last viable opportunity to reach the Muslim is between the service stage and fruition stage. After that they are too far indoctrinated for Christianity to appeal to them.

The fruition stage is the most difficult stage in which to reach Black Muslims. This is where it all comes together for them. Their philosophies become concrete and their theology is sound. They become intellectuals in this stage. They would probably die for the Nation when they reach this stage.

In this stage Black Muslims learn to deal with their hatred of the white man, although they have not changed their position.

There are some basic understandings one

must have to witness to Black Muslims.

NOTE THE FOLLOWING:

1. A white man will have very little success in dealing with Black Muslims, simply because he is white.

2. A Black Man who denies or is not aware of the social conditions that plague the Black Community will have very little success in dealing with Muslims.

3. Christianity as it is practiced in America, in general, is not religion as Jesus Christ intended.

4. People who do not belong to the status quo are not treated equally in America despite the color of their skin. This is especially true toward Black people.

5. Christian Theology and history have been taught from a European perspective. It perpetuates insensitivity to the needs of Black people and omits any acknowledgment of their contribution to society and presence in the Bible.

6. The public school system only provides true learning for the status quo. Black people educated in such a system are at a disadvantage. They do not have similar learning styles. Society penalizes them for this and considers them inferior. The truth is they are victims of an environ-

ment for learning that is not conducive to the African people.

7. White people are subconsciously taught at a young age that they are superior to Black people and taught to hate Black people. Most don't even know why they teach this to their children. They also don't know why they hate and why they are uncomfortable around Black people.

Black Muslims and Christians have different approaches to society. The Christian believes it is his duty to live in present society under these conditions. The Muslims reject the society and builds his own society by encouraging the support of Muslim owned and operated businesses. Some Christians believe poverty is spiritual and wealth is evil. The Muslim sees economic freedom as a basic right and wishes to attain that right totally independent from white society. If a Christian Black Man attempts to approach a Black Muslim with no knowledge of these elements of society, he will never reach the Black Muslim where he is.

chapter 5

Reaching Out

The greatest lesson taught for reaching out was taught by the Greatest Teacher, Jesus Christ. Ellen White says, "Christ's method alone will give true success in reaching the people. The Saviour mingled with men as one who desired their good. He showed His sympathy for them, ministered to their needs, and won their confidence. Then He bade them, 'Follow Me'" (Ministry of Healing, p. 143).

Philip Samaan, offers commentary on this statement in his book Christ's Way of Reaching People. He pulls out the five steps from this statement and expounds. The steps are as follows: mingling, sympathizing, ministering, winning and bidding. This is an excellent model for witnessing. You should use these steps in reaching Black Muslims. Look at them in more detail.

MINGLING AS ONE DESIRING THEIR GOOD. It is hard for anyone to mingle with someone who is not like them. People do not accept strangers with new ideas very often. Dr. Samaan suggests that it would be easier to mingle with those you see on a daily basis. The Prison Chaplain will contact many Muslims in the prison system. It would be advisable for him not to challenge any Muslim that he has not mingled with for a considerable period of time. He must first get to know him as a person and not just as a prisoner. If you can understand what makes a person laugh, cry, mad and happy, you will have a better chance in mingling with them comfortably. This will open the doors for other opportunities to witness.

Don't rush it. This is not a whimsical duty. Take the necessary time and patience to make it effective. Muslims are suspicious of the white man and any one who represents the white man. Muslims look to see if your skin is black but they also look to see if your mind is black. If you don't "desire the good of the people" then you cannot mingle with Black Muslims.

SYMPATHIZE WITH THEM. Be careful with this phrase. Muslims are not looking for anyone's sympathy. This kind of sympathy should not be confused with feeling sorry for the Black Man because of the evils against him.

When we sympathize with Muslims it is going to come down to one simple question. This question from the Black Muslims is "are you with us, or against us?" This is the most pertinent question in the Muslim mind. He will watch how you react to the social issues discussed as you mingle. If you cannot honestly take a stand on issues that plague the Black Man, then you have no business witnessing to Black Muslims.

When Jesus ministered to the poor he didn't say "you know its really a shame what kind of life you have to live, but it will get better." This is not sympathizing. Jesus was the True Sympathizer. He felt the pain of poverty, for he was poor. He knew what it meant to have to work for little or no wages. Jesus could relate to a conspiracy, for it was a conspiracy that led him to Calvary's tree. Jesus understands oppression and hatred, for he "came unto his own and his own received him not".

Jesus was the Chief Sufferer, and the Muslims receive that very well. They see Jesus as very much related to the Black Man and his suffering. They do, however, reject Jesus as God, because they believe that God could not suffer at the hand of evil. They cannot conceive the idea that God could be killed. What they need to understand is that Jesus did not have his life taken from him. The scriptures make that clear. "Therefore doth my Father love me, because I lay down my life, that I might take it again. No man taketh it from me, but I lay it down of myself. I have power to lay it down, and I have power to take it again" (John 10:17).

Black Liberation Theology proponents understand the reality of the African people's suffering. Some, however, struggle with loving the perceived oppressor. Those who harbor hatred for the oppressor are not prepared to witness to Muslims.

The response to suffering is similar for the Christian and the Black Muslim. Both look forward to the destruction of the wicked. The Christian looks for that and redemption of the righteous. The Muslim claims the things of the world. Christians understand that they are not of this world. Muslims are interested in the here and now, the Christian is interested in the hereafter. According to Black Muslims, Allah cannot save the white man because he is inherently evil and cannot be saved. To the Christian... "all have sinned and come short of the glory of God" (Romans 3:23).

The Christian witness should know that many white people have participated in the oppression of Blacks. Oppression is sin and oppressors need liberation for salvation. Without this understanding they could never reach a commonality with Black Muslims.

MINISTER TO THEIR NEEDS. This is where the proverbial rubber meets the road. If you have reached this point in your witnessing to Muslims, the practical side of the ministry will confront you. Your challenge will be an attitude that says "if you care so much, what have you done for me lately?" Ministering to the needs of the people and empowering their people to be independent of the white power structure is synonymous to the Muslims. An occasional brush with poverty does not make it ministry.

One of the greatest needs in the Black Community is jobs. There are few jobs in the Black Community that require any real training. Fast food restaurants are always hiring but this kind of work is often equated with slavery, or menial labor. It does very little for the self-esteem. Many people in the Black Community are working these minimum wage jobs.

It is different in other communities because in other communities the young people who work in menial labor are mostly working to learn responsibility. They don't have to work to pay bills. They are only working to pass the time and to get some spending money. In the Black Community people need jobs to pay the bills. They take any job they can get because they are not prepared for higher paying jobs.

Muslims don't have this problem because they provide jobs for their own. But if a Muslim needed a job desperately most would rather be unemployed than to work for the white man because it has been proven that they will not be treated fairly. Black Men with equal training as white men make less money and work longer and harder for promotions.

The needs of a Muslim will vary depending on what stage of his development he is in. A Muslim is not a real Muslim just because he discarded his "slave name" and changed it to an Arabic or African name. Unless he is in the fruition stage, where he has dealt with his emotions, we don't consider them true Muslims.

This can be seen by paralleling the Christian experience to the Islamic one. There are people who claim Christianity but are not dedicated to living a life free from sin. The same is true for Islam. Many claim it because it is socially acceptable. Discovering the Black Muslim's stage of religious experience will be an aid when trying to figure out how to minister to his needs.

WIN THEIR CONFIDENCE. Winning one's confidence is not easy. Just as you would deal with any other person, be yourself. Don't try to pretend that you know a lot about the Muslim religion. Very few people know a lot about it because it has been a mystery. Just let it flow naturally. They can tell what kind of books you have read and with whom you have been talking.

It is never wise to push your way into any conversation with Muslims. It takes time to win the confidence of a stranger, so get to know the person. Don't think that you will go through these steps in a matter of hours. It may take months to go through these steps.

INVITE THEM TO FOLLOW CHRIST. This is the purpose for the commission. This is the whole duty of the Christian. No matter if you are witnessing to a Muslim or a Bhuddist or an atheist, eventually you must invite them to follow Christ. Jesus said, "...if I be lifted up...I will draw all men unto me" (John 12:32). It is not our job to draw men to Christ. But we do have to participate in the process. Our participation is vital. We have to sharpen our skills to do it properly.

chapter 6

Conclusion

Knowing the people you relate to is very important in witnessing to them. Very few Christians demonstrated any interest in the Black Muslims. Outlined below is what the Muslims say about themselves. This outline is presented in each issue of the *Final Call*, the official newsletter of the Nation of Islam.

THE MUSLIM PROGRAM

What Do Muslims Want? This is the question asked most frequently by both the whites and the Blacks. The answers to this question shall be stated as simply as possible.

1. We want freedom. We want a full and complete freedom.

2. We want justice. Equal justice under the law. We want justice applied equally to all, regardless of creed or class or color.

3. We want equality of opportunity. We want equal membership in society with the best in

civilized society.

4. We want our people in America whose parents or grandparents were descendants from slaves, to be allowed to establish a separate state or territory of their own—either on this continent or elsewhere. We believe that our former slave masters are obligated to provide such land and that the area must be fertile and rich in minerals. We believe that our former slave masters are obligated to maintain and supply our needs in this separated territory for the next 20 to 25 years-until we are able to produce and supply our own needs.

Since we cannot get along with them in peace and equality, after giving them 400 years of our sweat and blood and receiving in return some of the worst treatment human beings have ever experienced, we believe our contributions to this land and the suffering forced upon us by white America, justifies our demand for complete separation in a state or territory of our own.

5. We want freedom for all Believers of Islam now held in federal prisons. We want freedom for all Black Men and women now under death sentence in innumerable prisons in the North as well as the South.

We want every Black Man and woman to have the freedom to accept or reject being separated from the slave master's children and establish a land of their own.

We know that the above plan for the solution of the Black and white conflict is the best and only answer to the problem between two people.

6. We want an immediate end to the police brutality and mob attacks against the so-called Negro throughout the United States.

We believe that the Federal government should intercede to see that Black Men and women tried in white courts receive justice in accordance with the laws of the land or allow us to build a new nation for ourselves, dedicated to justice, freedom and liberty.

7. As long as we are not allowed to establish a state or territory of our own, we demand not only equal justice under the laws of the United States, but equal employment opportunities—NOW!

We do not believe that after 400 years of free or nearly free labor, sweat and blood, which has helped America become rich and powerful, that so many thousands of Black people should have to subsist on relief, charity or live in poor houses.

8. We want the government of the United states to exempt our people from ALL taxation as long as we are deprived of equal justice under the

laws of the land.

9. We want equal education—but separate schools up to 16 for boys and 18 for girls on the condition that the girls be sent to women's colleges and universities. We want all Black children educated, taught and trained by their own teachers.

Under such a schooling system we believe we will make a better nation of people. The United States government should provide all necessary text books and equipment, schools and college buildings. The Muslim teachers shall be left free to teach and train their people in the way of righteousness, decency and self respect.

10. We believe that intermarriage or race mixing should be prohibited. We want the religion of Islam taught without hindrance or suppression.

These are some of the things that we, the Muslims, want for our people in North America.

WHAT THE MUSLIMS BELIEVE

1. We believe In the One God Whose proper name is Allah.

2. We believe in the Holy Qur'an and in the Scriptures of all the Prophets of God.

3. We believe in the truth of the Bible, but we believe that it has been tampered with and must be reinterpreted so that mankind will not be snared by

the falsehoods that have been added to it.

4. We believe in Allah's Prophets and the Scriptures they brought to the people.

5. We believe in the resurrection of the dead-not in physical resurrection-but in mental resurrection. We believe that the so-called Negroes are most in need of mental resurrection; therefore, they will be resurrected first.

Furthermore, we believe we are the people of God's choice, as it has been written, that God would choose the rejected and the despised. We can find no other persons fitting this description in these last days more than the so-called Negroes in America. We believe in the resurrection of the righteous.

6. We believe in the judgment; we believe this first judgment will take place as God revealed, in America...

7. We Believe this is the time in history for the separation of the so-called Negroes and the so-called white Americans. We believe the Black Man should be freed in name as well as in fact. By this we mean that he should be freed from the names imposed upon him by his former slave masters. Names which identified him as being the slave master's slave. We believe that if we are free indeed, we should go in our own people's names-

the Black people of the Earth.

8. We believe in justice for all, whether in God or not; we believe as others, that we are due equal justice as human beings. We believe in equality as a nation of equals. We do not believe that we are equal with our slave masters in the status of "freed slaves."

We recognize and respect American citizens as independent peoples and we respect their laws which govern this nation.

9. We believe that the offer of integration is hypocritical and is made by those who are trying to deceive the Black peoples into believing that their 400-year-old open enemies of freedom, justice and equality are, all of a sudden, their "friends." Furthermore, we believe that such deception is intended to prevent Black people from realizing that the time in history has arrived for the separation from the whites of this nation.

If white people are truthful about their professed friendship toward the so-called Negro, they can prove it by dividing up America with their slaves

We do not believe that America will ever be able to furnish enough jobs for her own millions of unemployed, in addition to jobs for the 20,000,000 Black people as well.

10. We believe that we who declare ourselves to be righteous Muslims, should not participate in wars which take the lives of humans. We do not believe this nation should force us to take part in such wars, for we have nothing to gain from it unless America agrees to give us the necessary territory wherein we may have something to fight for.

11. We believe our women should be respected and protected as the women of other nationalities are respected and protected.

12. We believe that Allah (God) appeared in the Person of Master W. Fard Muhammad, July 1930; the long-awaited "Messiah" of the Christians and the "Mahdi" of the Muslims.

We believe further and lastly that Allah is God and besides HIM there is no God and He will bring about a universal government of peace wherein we all can live in peace together.

—reprinted by permission from The Final Call; vol. 15, no. 9, 1996

God calls us to witness to all people and people groups. The message of the good news of Jesus Christ is for all mankind. We must reach everyone in our neighborhoods including Black Muslims. It will take much more than we have here. We feel that we have only scratched the surface. That's why this book is called an Introduction. It will take much more time, study and tact to win the followers of Allah to accept Jesus Christ as Lord and Saviour of their lives. It is, however, a task that is possible. We must continue to pray and continue to contact Muslims in order to improve on what little we already know.

When Christ delivered his final message to the apostles, after his resurrection, he told them that they would receive power to evangelize the entire world. Of course they could not comprehend the magnitude of his message, but in faith they trusted his promise. After Pentecost they became aware of the awesome power of the Holy Spirit to reach all humanity. Nothing has changed since the message and the commission remains the same. We must claim the promise of the risen Saviour and lead the lost sheep safely back to the fold. To this end we reach out to our brothers and sisters of Islam and point them to the cross.

Bibliography

Carson, Clayton. *The FBI Files on Malcom X.* New York: Caroll and Graf Publishers, Inc., 1991.

Essien-Udom, E.U. *Black Nationalism.* Chicago: The University of Chicago Press, 1962.

Felder, Cain Hope. *Stony the Road We Trod.* Minneapolis: Augsburg Fortress, 1991.

Haley, Alex and Betty Shabazz. *The Autobiography of Malcom X.* New York: Ballentine Books, 1964.

Harris, James. *Pastoral Theology: a Black Church Perspective.* Minneapolis: Augsburg Fortress, 1990.

Lincoln, C. Eric. *The Black Muslims in America.* Westport, Connecticut: Green Wood Press, 1973.

Madhubuti, Haki. *Black Men.* Chicago: Third World Press, 1990.

Muhammad, Elijah. *The Message to the Blackman.* Newport News, Virginia: United Brothers Communications Systems, 1965.

Salley, Columbus, and Ronald Behn. *What Color is Your God?* Downers Grove, Illinois: InterVarsity Press, 1981.

Samaan, Philip. *Christ's Method of Reaching People.* Hagerstown, MD: Review and Herald Press, 1990.

Williams, Chancellor. *The Destruction of Black Civilization.* Chicago: Third World Press, 1987.

Wright, Bruce. *Black Robes, White Justice.* New York: Caroll Publishers, 1990.

Wright, Bruce. *Final Call* New York: Caroll Publishers, 1990.

FOOTNOTES

{1} Barret, David B., ed. *World Christian Encyclopedia.* (Nairobi: Oxford University Press, 1982).

{2} Barret.

{3} Essien-Udom, E.U. *Black Nationalism* (Chicago: The University of Chicago Press, 1962), 337.

{4} Lincoln, C. Eric. *The Black Muslims in America* (Westport, Connecticut: Green Wood Press, 1973), 103.

{5} Lincoln, xv.

{6} Muhammad, Elijah. *Message to the Black Man in America* (Newport News, Virginia: United Brothers Communication Systems, 1965), 32.

{7} Wright, Bruce. *Black Robes, White Justice.* (New York: Carrol Publishers, 1990).